OCS Report
MMS 97-0004

Deepwater in the Gulf of Mexico:
America's New Frontier

U.S. Minerals Management Service

I0428083

Prepared By:
Deborah Cranswick
James Regg

U.S. Department of the Interior
Minerals Management Service
Gulf of Mexico OCS Region

February 1997
New Orleans

Deepwater in the Gulf of Mexico: America's New Frontier

Minerals Management Service

Executive Summary

This paper describes the extent and types of oil and gas exploration and development activities that are taking place in the deepwater portion of the Gulf of Mexico Outer Continental Shelf (OCS). The impacts on the workload and demands on the Minerals Management Service (MMS), particularly the Gulf of Mexico OCS Regional Office, as a result of deepwater activities are just beginning to occur. The full magnitude of the impacts is not yet known, although some specific impacts are emerging and others can be anticipated.

Favorable economics, the development of three-dimensional (3D) and subsalt geophysical technologies, the announcement of several deepwater discoveries, the development of new deepwater drilling and development technologies, the passage of the Deep Water Royalty Relief Act, and the opportunity to lease new prospects have all contributed to the revitalization of exploration and development in the Gulf of Mexico. After the recent implementation of deepwater royalty relief measures, specifically designed to support the development and production of deepwater tracts, the MMS received record bids in both 1996 lease sales. In 1994 and 1995, there were 210 blocks leased in 900 meters (approximately 3,000 feet) or greater water depth; in the 1996 sales, there were 712 blocks leased in that water depth.

Deepwater operations are significantly different from conventional operations in shallower waters of the shelf. Deepwater operations are significantly farther from shore, encounter different environmental conditions, are technologically more sophisticated, may produce at much higher rates, and are subject to different economic determinants. These differences will significantly impact the MMS Gulf Region's workload and present many technical and regulatory challenges.

The number and complexity of Exploration Plans, Development Operations Coordination Documents, pipeline applications, applications for permits to drill, and requests for regulatory departures or alternative compliance will continue to increase. In addition, the MMS has established requirements for the submittal of Deepwater Operations Plans and Conservation Information in support of proposed deepwater operations. New and evolving technologies, larger and more complex facilities, modifications of procedures, and additional environmental protection issues are all anticipated for deepwater activities. The MMS technical, safety, and environmental reviews of these proposed deepwater activities will take longer and require new expertise. The MMS is working diligently to keep pace with the evolving deepwater issues and technical expertise, and has developed the regulatory framework required to be an effective manager and regulator of these deepwater areas.

The challenges of effectively managing and regulating exploration and development activities in the frontier deepwater areas are in addition to ever-increasing demands of the OCS Program in the shallower water areas of the Gulf.

Table of Contents

Figures

Tables

Deepwater in the Gulf of Mexico: America's New Frontier

Minerals Management Service

Introduction

The purpose of this paper is to describe the extent and types of oil and gas exploration and development activities that are taking place in the deepwater portion of the Gulf of Mexico Outer Continental Shelf (OCS) (see Figure 1). (Within this report, unless otherwise noted, "deepwater" refers to water depths greater than 1,000 feet or 305 meters.) These activities are then considered in relation to the effects they will have on the operations and workload of the Minerals Management Service (MMS). Although the pace of deepwater activities has accelerated rapidly, the impacts to the MMS are just beginning. While the bulk of the workload for deepwater development will fall to the Gulf of Mexico Regional Office, staff loads, both technical and administrative, have and will show an increase in the headquarters and royalty management offices of MMS as well. The full magnitude of the impacts is not yet known, although some specific impacts are emerging and others can be anticipated.

For 50 years, oil and natural gas have been produced from the OCS underlying the Gulf of Mexico. This production represents more than 83 percent of total OCS oil production and more than 99 percent of all OCS natural gas production. In 1995, production from this area accounted for 15 percent of all oil produced in the U.S. and 26 percent of the natural gas (see Table 1). To date, most of the Gulf's production has come from fields located in relatively shallow waters. A new era for the Gulf of Mexico has begun with the intense interest in the oil and gas potential of the deepwater areas.

Table 1. 1995 U.S. Oil and Gas Production		
Source	Oil (barrels)	Gas (thousand cubic feet)
U.S. Domestic Production	2,394,400,000	18,902,000,000
Total OCS Production	429,190,000	5,015,000,000
Gulf of Mexico OCS	356,759,337	4,952,335,754
Deepwater Gulf of Mexico	47,169,705	196,723,756
Pacific OCS	72,430,663	62,664,246

A long, slow decline had been forecast for production from the Gulf of Mexico because it was thought that all of the most-promising shallow-water fields had already been found and were approaching or past their peak production levels. Recently, however, this perception has changed

Figure 1. The Gulf of Mexico Outer Continental Shelf. (Index map)

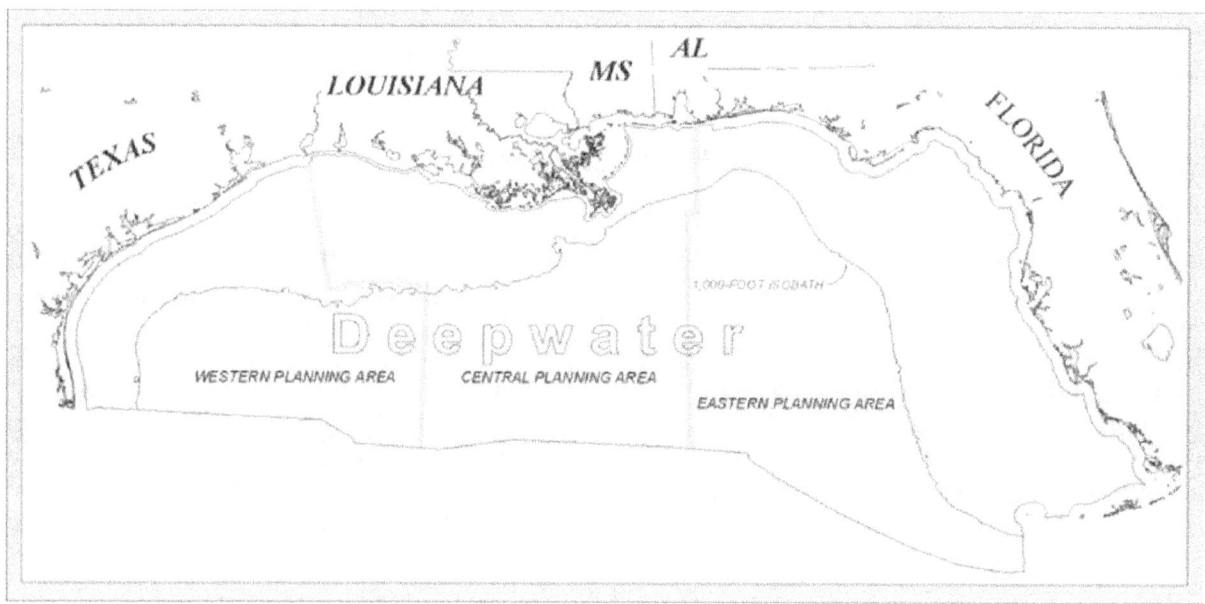

Figure 1. The Gulf of Mexico Outer Continental Shelf.

markedly. Due largely to a combination of favorable economics, recent discoveries in the deepwater shelf and slope regions of the Gulf, availability of infrastructure, deepwater royalty relief, the opportunity to lease new prospects, and the use of new technology to extend the life of current fields and accurately find new ones, the Gulf of Mexico OCS is once again the scene of a relatively intense search for new oil and gas fields. This turnabout is concentrated in the Central and Western Planning Areas of the Gulf of Mexico. Production from the Gulf of Mexico OCS is expected to increase dramatically over the next four years. By the year 2000, oil production is forecast to increase by as much as 70-100 percent. The MMS Gulf of Mexico Region projects an increase in oil production from 0.9 million barrels per day to as much as 1.7-1.9 million barrels per day. The MMS projects that gas production will remain fairly steady or increase from 13.9 billion cubic feet per day in 1995 to as much as 17.2 billion cubic feet per day in 2000.

The technology employed by the offshore industry to find and develop oil and gas changes significantly in deeper waters beyond the shelf edge. Over the past several years, the results of industry's search for deepwater prospects have appeared in press releases, journals, and newsletter articles. The tone of the media reports reflects the intense interest of the oil and gas industry and the enthusiasm of support industries. Deepwater development represents new economic opportunities for many companies and individuals both in the Gulf of Mexico coastal zone and beyond.

Deepwater operations differ from those conducted in the shallower waters in that they

- may be significantly more remote;
- may be subject to different environmental conditions;
- may be technologically more sophisticated;
- may produce at much higher rates; and
- are typically subject to different economic determinants.

Renewed industry activity and interest in the Gulf of Mexico have expanded the Regional Office's workload over the past few years, are anticipated to continue increasing workload over the next several years (see Table 2), and will have extensive repercussions on the efforts required by the MMS Gulf Regional Office to meet its mission responsibilities. The growth in workload will be attributable in part to the continued investigation and analysis of operating requirements for complex, technically advanced deepwater systems, and to the continued development of staff expertise to perform such analyses.

There are many unknowns in the deepwater area, both environmental and technical. Many regulations will have to be revised and new policies and guidance will need to be developed. Undoubtedly, a number of unanticipated issues or consequences that require new approaches or processes will surface as deepwater activities intensify. Emphasis on deepwater development and the associated innovative technology for drilling and production, as well as the need to address engineering, safety, and unique supplemental bonding issues, will present challenges to the Region's regulatory function. The major components of the MMS regulatory and environmental coordination and review process are outlined in Table 3.

3

Table 2. Gulf of Mexico OCS Activities FY 1992 - FY 1998

	FY 1992	FY 1993	FY 1994	FY 1995	FY 1996	FY 1997*	FY 1998*
Industry Activity							
Total Active Leases				5,000	5,196	6,500	8,300
Exploratory Wells Drilled	210	318	387	361	446	460	480
Plans of Exploration/Development	407	572	719	711	768	800	850
Deepwater Operations Plans	-	-	-	-	13	40	50
MMS Gulf of Mexico OCS Region Activity							
Environmental Assessments	203	231	198	145	236	245	260
Categorical Exclusion Reviews	733	927	1,143	1,138	1,196	1,350	1,500
Air Quality Reviews	355	602	1,148	1,255	998	1,400	1,600
Archaeological Reviews	488	406	648	664	740	900	1,000
Oil Spill Plan Reviews	589	851	752	879	604	1,100	1,200
Inspections	7,500	9,100	9,900	10,500	10,600	11,600	12,700
G&G Permits Processed	126	126	135	106	126	140	150

* projected

Table 3. Overview of MMS OCS Regulatory Compliance

Prelease Activities
- Review and approval of Geological and Geophysical Permits
- Adjudication actions (e.g., Qualification of Companies*, Equal Employment Opportunit y Certification*)

Leasing Activities
- Conducting lease sales (e.g., sale st atistics, seismic data acquisition, bid evaluation, issuing lease instruments)
- Adjudication actions (e.g., Bond Coverage*, De signation of Operator*, Certification of Financial Responsibility*, Lease Stipulations and Regulations)

Lease Exploration Activities
- Monitoring preliminary activities (e.g,. soil boring, 3D seismic surveying, shallow hazard s surveying, archaeological surveying, live bottom surveying)
- Technical, safety, and environmental reviews of plan s and applications (e.g., Plan of Exploration, Application for Permit to Drill, Hydrogen Sulfide Control Plan, Oil Spill Contingency Plan)
- Monitoring and inspections of drilling operations for exploratory and delineation wells (e.g. , Sundry Notice, Conditions to Drill, Final Location Report, Weekly Progress Reports, on-sit e inspections, Well Summary, Wel l Test Notification, Application for Well Producibility, Caisson Application, Plug and Abandonment)

Lease Development Activities
- Technical, safety, and environmental reviews of plans and applications (e.g., Developmen t Operations Coordination Document, Deepwater Operations Plan, Structure Application, Safety System Design and Instal lation, Application for Permit to Drill, Hydrogen Sulfide Control Plan, Oil Spill Contingency Plan, Pipeline Application)
- Monitoring and inspections of well drilling operations for production wells (e.g., Sundry Notice, Safety Device Training, Weekly Pr ogress Reports, Notice of Installation, Application for Permit to Drill)

Production Phase Activities
- Conservation and Rate Control (Unitization, Suspension of O perations, Suspension of Production, Maximum Efficient Rate, Maximum Production Rate, Gas Cap Production, Production withi n 500 feet of Lea se Line, Application to Commingle Production, Downhole Commingling, Meter Proving Reports, Royalty Meter Run Tickets,)
- Royalty Management (e.g., Liquid Hydrocarbon and Gas Measurement)
- Continuing monitoring and inspections of production operations (e.g., workovers, temporar y abandonment, annual inspections, erosion control program, disposal of wastes)
- Continuing adjudication actions (e.g., De signation of Operator, Assignments, Bonds, Mortgages)

Lease Termination Activities
- Technical, safety, and environmental reviews of plans and application s (e.g., Sundry Notices, plug and abandon wells, platform removal, site clearance, pipeline abandonment)
- Monitoring and inspections of abandonment operations
- Adjudication actions (e.g., lease relinquishment and termination, cancel certificate of financial responsibility)

*Many adjudication actions are performed repeatedly throughout the term of a lease.

Deepwater Activities and Trends

Many OCS activities reflect the trend toward increasing deepwater leasing, exploration, and development (see Appendix 1). Much of the information presented in this report has been publicly released by companies, reported by the industry trade press, or generated by the MMS. These data are subject to frequent updates.

Leasing Activities

Prelease

Although the number of deepwater geophysical permits issued by the MMS has remained relatively constant over the past five years, MMS anticipates an increase in the number of permit applications for deepwater geophysical surveys. Since the passage of deepwater royalty relief legislation, the geophysical surveying companies have indicated that they anticipate numerous speculative deepwater surveys. In addition, recent surveys cover larger areas, include more line-miles of data, and are in progressively deeper areas. State-of-the-art 3D seismic data have enabled industry to identify, with greater precision, where the most promising deepwater prospects are located. This 3D technology is being used in developed areas on the shallower shelf to identify bypassed hydrocarbon-bearing zones in currently producing formations and new productive horizons near or below currently producing formations. It is also being used in developed areas for reservoir monitoring and field management.

Leasing

For some time, industry had only a low-level interest in leasing in the deepwater areas in the Gulf of Mexico. Industry interest and leasing have escalated significantly since the passage of the Deep Water Royalty Relief Act (see Table 4). The Deep Water Royalty Relief Act (DWRRA) defines deepwater as greater than 200 m (656 ft), although for operational considerations in the Gulf, deepwater is greater than 305 m (1,000 ft). The DWRRA establishes three zones based on water depth for different levels of royalty relief: 200-400 meters, 400-800 meters, and greater than 800 meters. In 1995, the overall number of tracts bid on and later awarded leases (in water depths greater than 400 meters (1,312 feet)) multiplied fourfold (400%) from the average of the previous two years, and these deepwater leases accounted for 33 percent of all leases awarded. The 1996 Central Gulf of Mexico Sale 157 was the largest lease sale ever held in the Gulf of Mexico in terms of the number of tracts bid on and resulted in the addition of 430 leases in water depths greater than 400 meters. An additional 392 leases in water depths greater than 400 meters result from 1996 Western Gulf Sale 161.

To date, the most significant players in the Gulf's deepwater oil and gas arena have been the major oil companies. Shell Offshore has clearly been the leader. Other major companies (e.g., BP Exploration, Amoco, Mobil, Exxon, and Texaco) are actively increasing their lease holdings and drilling operations. Independents (e.g., Oryx, Enserch, CNG, Marathon, Conoco, BHP Petroleum, and Louisiana Land and Exploration) are also gaining a foothold as primary lease holders, particularly in the shallower sections of the deepwater Gulf, or as partners with major oil companies. Recent entrants include foreign-owned companies (e.g., Statoil (Norway) and Enterprise Oil (United Kingdom)). In addition, both major and independent companies have shown an increasing and renewed interest in the shallow areas of the Gulf.

Table 4. Gulf of Mexico OCS Lease Sales 1992-1996

Sale Number	Sale Date	Number of Companies Participating	Total Leases	Leasing by Water Depth Categories*							
				< 200 m		200-400 m		400-900 m		> 900 m	
				No.	%	No.	%	No.	%	No.	%
139	5/13/92	64	144	120	83%	4	3%	13	9%	7	5%
141	8/19/92	38	60	56	93%	0	0%	4	7%	0	0%
142	3/24/93	61	187	152	81%	5	3%	23	12%	7	4%
143	9/15/93	48	149	109	73%	10	7%	13	9%	17	11%
147	3/30/94	82	368	307	83%	7	2%	24	7%	30	8%
150	8/17/94	57	192	159	83%	18	9%	6	3%	9	5%
152	5/10/95	88	572	383	67%	18	3%	58	10%	113	20%
155	9/15/95	60	263	126	48%	34	13%	45	17%	58	22%
157**	4/24/96	93	902	444	49%	28	3%	38	4%	392	44%
161**	9/25/96	72	606	176	29%	38	3%	72	12%	320	53%

*Due to rounding. the percentages for water depth categories may not sum to 100%.
**Sales 157 and 161 were held after the enactment of the Deep Water Royalty Relief Act.

Exploration Activities

Plans and Permitting

Between 1992 and 1996, the number of submitted exploration and development plans almost doubled (see Table 2). The number of Applications for Permits to Drill deepwater wells in the Gulf of Mexico OCS approved by the MMS more than doubled between 1993 and 1995, from 41 to 85.

The MMS prepares environmental assessment documents (Categorical Exclusion Reviews or site-specific Environmental Assessments) for all plans for exploration and development and for pipeline applications. Environmental review and protection, as well as safety and technical review, in deepwater areas will present special challenges for the MMS. Fewer environmental studies have been conducted in the deeper water areas of the Gulf. The potential impacts of the technologies evolving to meet the requirements of deepwater exploration and development are not well known. Some of the issues that the MMS addresses in the safety, technical, and environmental reviews are

- new and unusual technologies;
- oil-spill contingency planning;
- sour-gas production;

- chemosynthetic communities;
- live bottom areas;
- pinnacle and other hard-bottom habitats;
- air quality;
- water quality;
- endangered and threatened species;
- pipeline tows and landfalls; and
- lease abandonment and decommissioning operations.

Drilling

Drilling rigs operating in the deep waters of the Gulf of Mexico more than quadrupled between 1991 and 1996, from an average of 4 rigs drilling monthly to 17 rigs. Drilling activities are currently constrained by the overall availability of rigs capable of working in these water depths, the availability of rig crews, and riser availability. Because of the number of attractive prospects in deepwater areas and increasingly favorable project economics, most deepwater rigs are already under long-term contracts with various oil and gas operators. Though there is some movement of deepwater rigs to the Gulf of Mexico from international waters, similar constraints in the international market limit the number of rigs that can be moved. Increasingly, the trend in the deepwater drilling market is the conversion and upgrade of other rigs or vessels to deepwater-drilling-capable rigs. A small number of new rigs are also under construction. (Conoco announced in October 1996 a joint venture to build a $200 million drillship that will be able to operate out to 10,000 feet water depth.) Very few of these conversions or new builds are speculative projects; most of these projects are under long-term contracts to oil and gas operators before construction even begins.

Discoveries

Discovery of OCS deepwater fields in the Gulf of Mexico began accelerating in 1994 (see Appendix 2). The vast majority of these discoveries have been in the Central Gulf offshore Louisiana and Mississippi (see Figure 2). Though Shell Offshore has been the pioneer in the deepwater Gulf, other companies have been quick to recognize the potential of this province as Shell began to show that there were indeed sizeable fields to be found. Shell's announcements of large discoveries in the Tahoe (1984), Bullwinkle (1985), Auger (1987), and Mars (1989) fields have heightened interest in this region. During the past two years, industry has announced plans to develop many of the recent deepwater discoveries (see Appendix 2) including Texaco's Petronius and Gemini prospects; Shell's Ram-Powell, Ursa, and Mensa prospects; Chevron's Genesis prospect; and BP's Troika and Marlin prospects.

Figure 2 Deepwater Discoveries (map)

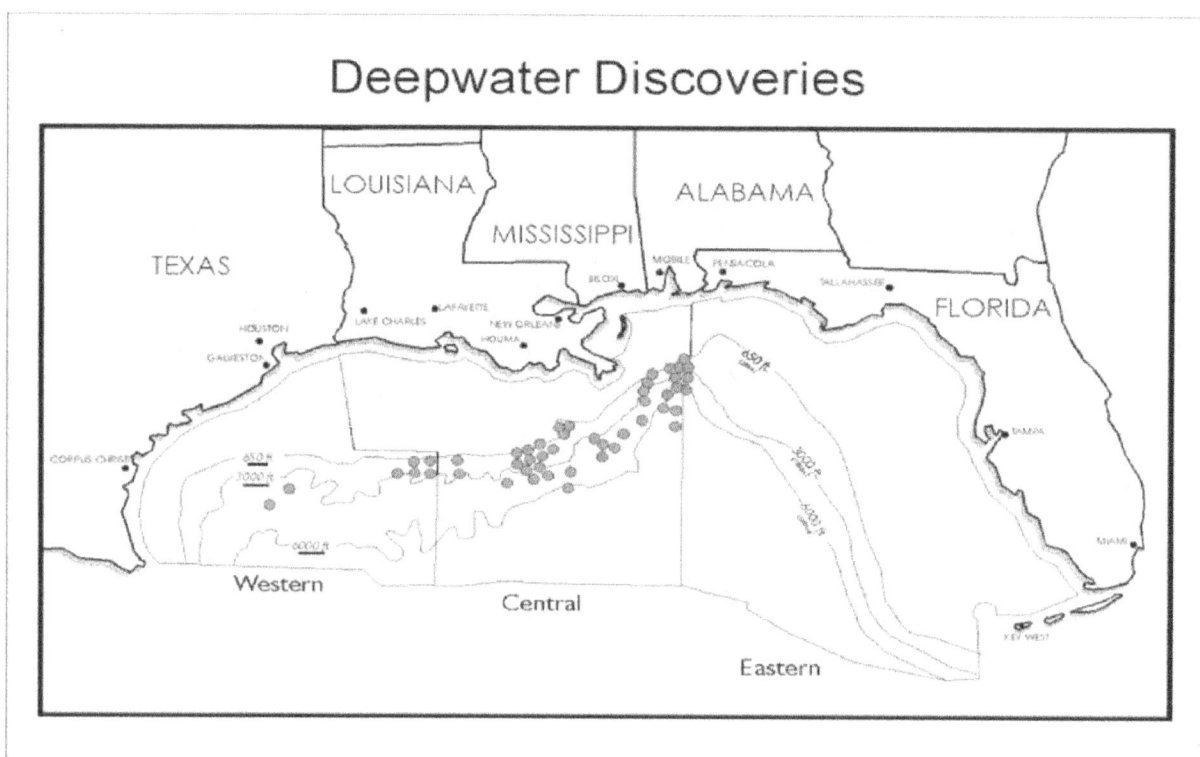

Production and Reserves

In 1995, the 47.2 million barrels of oil (MMBO) produced from deepwater Gulf of Mexico OCS prospects accounted for more than 14 percent of total Gulf OCS oil production; the 196.7 billion cubic feet (Bcf) of deepwater gas accounted for about 4 percent of total Gulf natural gas production (see Table 1). It is interesting to note that deepwater oil production increased 260 percent over the 5-year period 1992-1996; deepwater gas production increased 375 percent during this same period. During this same time, the number of producing deepwater fields more than tripled, from 5 to 18 fields.

Projections for Gulf of Mexico oil and gas production through 2000 range widely, depending on which assumptions are used. The most conservative projections are that oil production will increase 50 percent, to 1.45 MMBO per day. The MMS Gulf of Mexico Region projects an increase in oil production from 0.9 MMBO per day in 1995 to as much as 1.7-1.9 MMBO per day in 2000 and projects that gas production will remain fairly steady or increase from 13.9 Bcf per day to as much as 17.2 Bcf per day. A large portion of this additional production will be derived from new deepwater fields. Less dramatic, but still sizeable, contributions will be obtained from the development of the newly discovered subsalt plays.

During the period 1991-1995, the total number of deepwater fields with proven reserves increased more than 50 percent, from 13 to 20 fields. The MMS projects that the number of proved fields will grow another 80 percent by the year 2000 to 36 fields. In 1995, proved reserves in deepwater OCS fields under the Gulf of Mexico were estimated to be 1.131 billion barrels of oil (BBO) and 4.6 trillion cubic feet (Tcf) of gas. Recent projections indicate that by the year 2000 proved reserves of deepwater oil will more than double to 2.467 BBO and gas reserves will increase nearly 80 percent to 8.2 Tcf.

Technology

The 1,000-foot (305-meter) water depth barrier for installation of production platforms was broken in 1976 when Shell installed the Cognac platform in 1,025 feet of water (see Figure 3). This record was broken in 1989 by Shell's Bullwinkle platform at 1,353 feet and Conoco's Jolliet

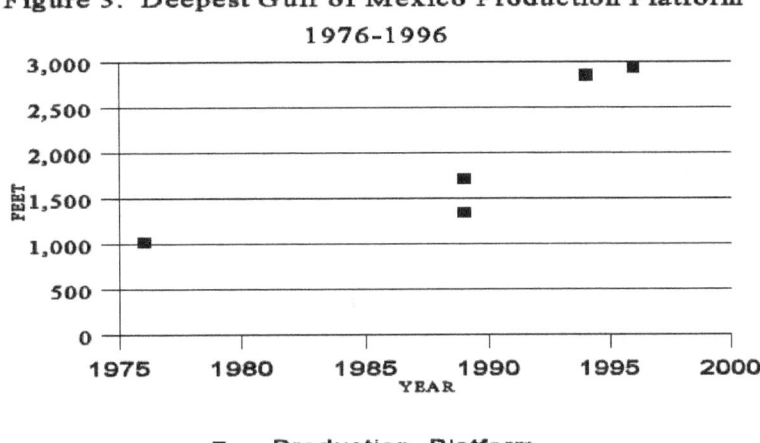

Figure 3. Deepest Gulf of Mexico Production Platform 1976-1996

platform, the first tension leg platform (TLP) in the Gulf, at 1,720 feet. Jolliet held the record until Auger was installed in 2,860 feet of water in 1994. Shell's Mars platform, located in 2,940 feet of water, assumed the current deepwater production record when it was installed in 1996.

Industry is rapidly advancing operations into deepwater (Appendix 2). Shell Offshore has announced its Ram-Powell prospect slotted for installation in 3,255-feet water depth with production start-up projected for 1997. Texaco's Gemini prospect in 3,393 feet of water is projected for production start-up in 2000. In even deeper water, production is planned for Shell's Ursa prospect at 4,021 feet, Texaco's Fuji prospect at 4,243 feet, Exxon's Diana at 4,657 feet, Shell's Mensa prospect at 5,376 feet, and Amoco's Kings Peak prospect at 6,530 feet. In 1996, the Baja well was drilled by Shell in approximately 7,600 feet of water.

In the future, even greater water depths will be tackled by industry. By the early 2,000's, exploration wells may be drilled at 10,000-foot depths, at the very limits of the Exclusive Economic Zone, and production systems will be designed for depths of 6,000 feet and greater.

The product pipeline networks for gas and oil will have been extended well off the continental shelf and down the continental slope. Large reservoirs will be serviced by tension leg platforms or SPAR platform derivatives with extended capability to handle distant subsea completions. These facilities will likely be operated by consortia of major oil companies. Smaller deepwater reservoirs will be produced by independent oil companies utilizing small moored floating platforms, many of which will be capable of reuse in other locations. The business climate will demand innovative platform configurations, reductions in the weight and cost of risers and mooring systems and solutions to the pipeline reliability problems.

In water depths exceeding 1,000 feet, the use of conventional, bottom-founded (fixed) platform design quickly becomes uneconomic. As new discoveries are made in deeper and deeper water, the innovative technologies used by industry to design and build deep-ocean compliant structures continue to evolve to meet technical and economic needs for deepwater development. Nonconventional production platforms, such as tension leg platforms, spars, and subsea completions (see Figure 4), are being utilized and new designs are constantly being researched and evaluated. This rapid evolution in technology needs to be independently verified to ensure continued safety of operations and protection of the environment. Within MMS, technical personnel review operational problems and consider possible technological solutions, which may be better defined through research efforts. The Technology Assessment and Research Program (TARP) of MMS funds research projects to provide a continuing and comprehensive technology base within the MMS to ensure that OCS operations are orderly, safe, and pollution-free, and to ensure that MMS regulatory requirements facilitate the use of advanced technologies.

Many deepwater platforms, pipelines, and subsea completion projects are currently under construction or awaiting start of construction, under design or planning, or under study (see Table 5). These newer designs have not only fostered the progression into deeper waters, but they have reduced overall construction and installation costs. Perhaps more importantly, they have reduced the cycle time from discovery to first production. Oryx/CNG's Neptune spar platform, the first of several spars already on order, realized significantly lower construction costs. With the transition from the "Auger" design to the "Mars" design, Shell cut the construction period to nine months, at a savings of $120 million. Since 1989, most of the deepwater development designs have involved the use of subsea completions connected to shallower-water fixed facilities or some variant of traditional production systems. Other options for handling and transporting deepwater production are also being explored, including deepwater "host" processing facilities,

12

multiphase pipelines, and tankering operations. The technology for installation of pipelines in deep waters has kept pace with the evolving technology for deepwater drilling and production systems. Between 1993 and 1995, the number of pipeline right-of-way and installation applications increased by more than 20 percent (see Figure 5). In 1996, a record number of pipeline miles was approved and installed. Many of the recently proposed pipelines are significantly longer than most pipelines installed in the past.

Figure 4 Deepwater Development Systems in the Gulf of Mexico (graphic)

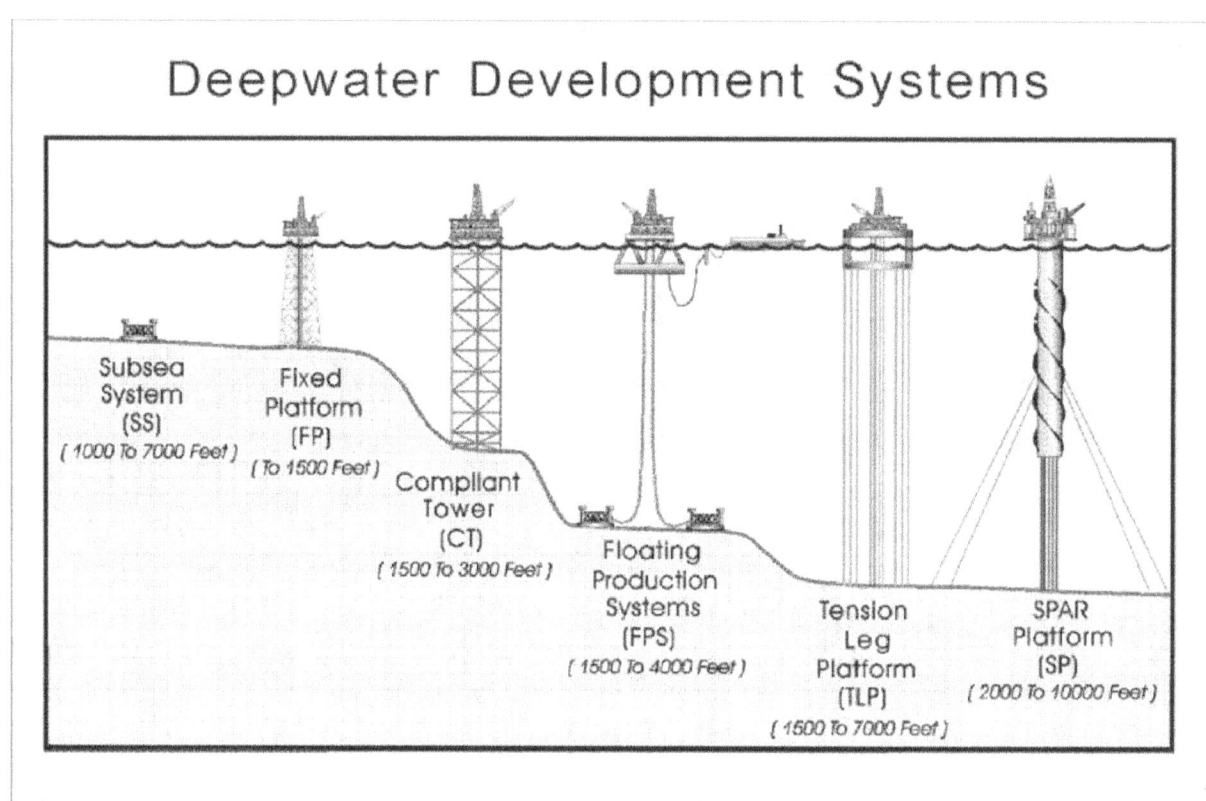

Table 5. Announced Gulf of Mexico Projects by Water Depth

Water Depth (approx. meters)	Under Construction/ Awaiting Start			Design/Planning Phase			Under Study			Total		
	PLA SUB	PIP		PLA SUB	PIP		PLA	PIP	SUB	PLA	PIP	SUB
0-100							9	11	4	72	153	5
100 - 200	19	6	1	44	136	0	5	6	3	13	20	6
200 - 300	3	1	0	5	13	3	4	7	3	7	13	5
300+	3	0	2	0	6	0	1	33	34	3	53	47
	2	3	3	0	17	10						
TOTAL	27	10	6	49	172	13	19	57	44	95	239	63

PLA = Platforms PIP = Pipelines SUB = Subsea completions
Source: *Gulf of Mexico Field Development Report, January 1997*, Offshore Data Services.

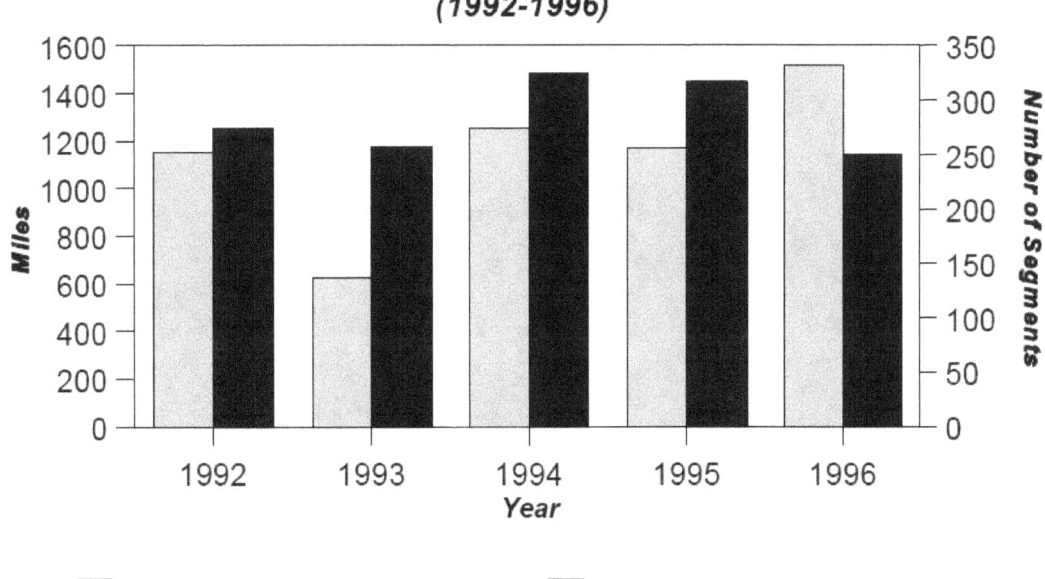

Figure 5. Gulf of Mexico Pipelines Approved (1992-1996)

Pipeline Miles (Y1)   Pipeline Segments (Y2)

Impact of Deepwater Activities on the MMS

Over time, the MMS Offshore Program has become increasingly complex. New issues, new laws and regulations, and new and expanding operations from deepwater exploration, discovery, and production have intensified the demands on the MMS. These have impacted many different parts of the MMS, but the greatest impact is on the Gulf of Mexico OCS Regional office--both in terms of workload and of expertise. Much of MMS's expertise has evolved around regulating the more traditional shelf-based oil and gas operations. Deepwater operations differ from those conducted in the shallower waters of the Gulf in that they

- may be significantly more remote. Most deepwater developments are located more than 100 miles from shore; some are as far as 200 miles. Many of these facilities will be beyond a 2-hour helicopter flight, and these larger, more complex facilities will require more detailed inspections and longer inspection times. The Auger platform is 172 miles from the Lafayette heliport and the Mensa project will be 120 miles from New Orleans. The Baja exploratory well was more than 150 miles from shore and required a special contract helicopter to transport MMS drilling inspectors to the site;

- may be subject to substantially different environmental conditions. Bottom conditions and associated benthic communities in these areas are relatively unknown. Additional environmental studies will be required, developing informed and comprehensive environmental assessments will be more difficult, and new mitigation measures may need to be developed. Pipelines for deepwater developments will be substantially longer, possibly encountering various habitats and geologic hazards, thus complicating the safety, technical, and environmental analyses and environmental protection associated with these projects;

- may be technologically more sophisticated. The challenges of deepwater exploration and development have promoted the development of new technologies. New drilling vessels, production systems, and nonconventional production platforms are being used. Many developments will use subsea completions with computerized remote control systems;

- may produce at much higher rates. One of the features of deepwater discoveries that have made them so attractive is the high individual well rates. The record for sustained rate from an individual well is 13,000 barrels of oil per day (BOPD) by a well on Shell's Platform Auger, but even higher rates have been already reached on a temporary basis (15,000 BOPD) at the Mars facility. Only a few years ago the Gulf had only a few wells that produced at a rate of 5,000 barrels a day or greater. Loss of control of such a well presents proportionately greater potential impacts to the environment than would a less remote, lesser-rate well;

- are typically subject to different economic determinants. The MMS will need to conduct increasingly sophisticated analyses on both the primary and associated nearby reservoirs tapped by deepwater development to ensure that smaller, but still economic, reservoirs are developed. If larger fields are developed and the facilities removed, then development of smaller nearby fields may be delayed or may not occur.

Deepwater operations present many challenges including identifying risk and incorporating that risk into permitting decisions. Another challenge will be evaluating and mitigating potential adverse environmental impacts. The MMS is working diligently to keep pace with evolving deepwater issues and technical expertise, and is continuously developing the regulatory framework required to manage risk effectively. These efforts will allow the MMS to be an effective manager and regulator of these deepwater areas. On regulatory issues, the MMS has

- formed an internal Deepwater Workgroup in 1992 composed of Regional and Headquarters staff to address technical issues and regulatory concerns relating to deepwater operations. As a result of this team's efforts, new regulatory requirements have been developed for the submittal of Deepwater Operations Plans (DWOP) for operations in greater than 1,000 feet (305 meters) of water and for all projects using subsea completion technology (Notice to Lessees (NTL) 96-4N). The DWOP is intended to provide the MMS with the information needed to evaluate the new deepwater operations and reduce industry apprehensions by giving the MMS an early enough look to highlight significant concerns before investments are made;

- participated in the industry-led DeepStar project. The Gulf of Mexico Region continues to work with DeepStar to stay current with the rapidly evolving technology used in deepwater development and production, and to identify and address regulatory issues in advance or permitting decisions;

- performed extensive regulatory and technical review for subsea completion technology;

- issued NTL 96-6N (effective October 1, 1996) on submittal of Conservation Information (reservoir and geologic) for deepwater or subsea development projects; and

- begun developing a new NTL to address concerns on production within 500 feet (150 meters) of lease lines and on regulating high-volume horizontal wells for all OCS leases.

Although the full impact on the Region is not known because new technologies are being developed and applied in the field, and new issues are expected to arise, some specific impacts are emerging and others can be anticipated.

Leasing Activities

Geological and Geophysical Permitting

With the implementation of deepwater royalty relief and the record-breaking number of bids at the 1996 Gulf of Mexico lease sales, the geophysical companies have committed to large speculative 2D and 3D geophysical surveys in deepwater areas. The MMS is working to keep abreast of the new developments in deepwater seismic surveying technologies. The number of Geological and Geophysical Permits has been consistently high over the last five years (see Table 6) and the number of permit applications is expected to increase. Current surveys are incorporating denser grids with more line-miles of data, are covering larger areas, and are moving out into progressively deeper water. The workload involved in the review and issuance of these permits is increasing. In the coming years, MMS will acquire these much needed modern data sets, which are necessary for fair market valve determinations and for reserves and resource analyses of deepwater fields.

**Table 6. Geological and Geophysical Exploration Permits
in the Gulf of Mexico 1992-1996**

Calendar Year	GULF OF MEXICO OCS			
	LOUISIANA	TEXAS	MAFLA[1]	TOTAL
1992	103 (46)	27 (5)	4 (2)	134 (53)
1993	102 (56)	29 (11)	4 (1)	135 (68)
1994	91 (36)	41 (17)	3	135 (53)
1995	78 (35)	27 (12)	0	105 (47)
1996	94 (40)	36 (13)	1 (1)	131 (54)
Total	468 (213)	160 (58)	12 (4)	640 (275)

[1] Mississippi, Alabama, and Florida
(Numbers in parenthesis indicate permits issued for 3-D seismic exploration as part of total permits issued.)

Resource Estimates and Exploration/Development Projections

Prior to each lease sale, the Gulf Region's Office of Resource Evaluation develops resource estimates and projects exploration and development (E&D) activities associated with both the proposed lease sale and the OCS Program in the Gulf of Mexico. Theses estimates and projections use the most recent National Assessment as a starting point, and then make projections based on MMS geological, geophysical, and engineering analyses, on statistical analysis of past OCS activities and production, and on economic information and projections. Because the majority of the impact producing factors assessed in the E&D have historically occurred in shallow water, it has become necessary to assess new technologies and techniques for exploration, development, and production. The E&D projections must incorporate new development scenarios, more extreme environmental factors, new deepwater plays, different reservoir characteristics (including significantly higher production rates), higher facility and operational costs, and different economic factors (for example, the Deep Water Royalty Relief Act). The need for ongoing analysis of emerging deepwater trends and technologies will continue to grow.

Environmental Studies

The Environmental Studies Program (ESP) is responsible for providing the research and environmental information necessary for decisionmakers to make informed decisions on OCS activities.

The MMS environmental studies are designed to address specific issues relating to the environmental and socioeconomic health of the region, both before and after OCS leasing. Since most MMS-funded studies have been done on the continental shelf out to 1,000 feet of water, the ESP will be heavily affected as new information needs are identified. In response to the need to identify the implications of deepwater activities quickly, the MMS is sponsoring a Deepwater Workshop in April 1997 to pull together experts who will attempt to identify and prioritize the most critical technical and environmental data needs to aid deliberations for both project and manpower planning, and budget purposes. Significant biological and physical indices must be identified and monitored. Baseline or reconnaissance studies are also needed.

Since the mid-1980's, studies of the deep-sea in general, and chemosynthetic communities and marine mammals in particular, have been funded and completed. Toward the end of the initial Gulf deep-sea research program, chemosynthetic communities were discovered in the Gulf in water depths from about 500 to 1,000 meters (1,640 to 3,281 feet). Subsequent specialized studies were conducted on chemosynthetic ecosystems at selected sites to determine the distribution, abundance, function, productivity, and vulnerability of these communities. Restrictions on OCS operations were developed to protect these sensitive communities and a Notice to Lessees and Operators (NTL 88-11) was issued in 1988. Additional follow-up chemosynthetic community studies are needed, and are planned, to determine the rate of change in these communities. In addition, studies on the distribution and abundance of marine mammals in the Gulf of Mexico, particularly in deepwater, are ongoing.

Onshore facilities and infrastructure to support deepwater activities may have widespread effects on Gulf coast socioeconomic conditions. The study "A Socioeconomic Analysis of Port Expansion at Port Fourchon" was just awarded to document the growth of OCS-support activities in the Port Fourchon, Louisiana area. This study will also develop a model of the economy of the area that will allow the projection of future economic effects of OCS activities. Other studies on these potential impacts, and on the potential impacts to water quality, air quality, and wetlands, are in the planning stages.

As OCS operations move into deeper waters, the ultimate fate of deepwater structures is being studied. Below some water depth, the amount of fishes associated with offshore platforms may decrease to a negligible amount. There are limited data regarding this critical water depth, which could be an important consideration for abandonment options. Information about the possible limitation to the artificial reef effect and the distribution patterns of fishes is needed to effectively manage and regulate facility abandonment at deepwater sites.

Headquarters environmental staff are involved in these new research areas and priorities, because all such initiatives must be managed in the larger context to ensure full coordination and the broader perspective. A change in both short-term and long-term research schedules also must be budgeted for, not an easy task in today's competitive climate. The administrative load of more research projects, new issues, and shifting priorities will have a noticeable impact on the ESP staff loads in the coming years.

Lease Sale Environmental Impact Statements

A comprehensive Environmental Impact Statement (EIS) is prepared for each Gulf of Mexico OCS lease sale. The EIS analyzes both the potential impacts of the proposed lease sale and the comprehensive impacts of the OCS Program. As MMS projected a dramatic move toward development in deepwater, major revisions were made in the focus and scenario of the lease sale

EIS's to account for the differences inherent in deepwater operations as compared with operations on the shelf.

Due to the technological changes associated with deepwater exploration and development activities and the associated transportation schemes, additional resources will need to be allocated to deepwater scenario development and analysis for use in lease sale EIS's. Various exploration, development, production, and transportation options must be considered and potential impacts resulting from each option evaluated. New and evolving technologies, longer and larger diameter pipelines with additional associated landfalls, increased production rates, and possible new abandonment and site clearance procedures must be incorporated into the EIS scenario. Projections of these factors and the potential associated impacts must be fully addressed in the EIS. New environmental resources may be discovered in deepwater areas, and any potential impacts to these resources from OCS activities would need to be analyzed. Development of mitigation measures for new and different potential impacts from deepwater operations is an ongoing process. Monitoring mitigation compliance and effectiveness is becoming an increasingly important and resource-demanding part of the Gulf Region's mission.

The MMS is conducting extensive scoping to identify alternatives to the proposed lease sales, for issues associated with deepwater activities, and for possible mitigation for potential impacts associated with deepwater activities. The alternatives, issues, and mitigating measures identified will be addressed in lease sale EIS's. Socioeconomic impacts to the coastal zone from expanding and deepening ports facilities have already been identified as a significant issue associated with deepwater development. Significantly increased efforts will be needed to fully understand and evaluate these impacts.

Lease Administration and Adjudication

Administrative workloads in lease administration are expected to escalate over the next several years due to the upsurge in deepwater activities, the overall expansion of industry activity in the Gulf, and the increasing size of Gulf of Mexico lease sales (see Table 4). Once leases are listed, records related to the assignment of record title interest, operating rights, mortgages, and production status must be maintained for the life of the lease. Management of official lease files and associated documents will require more time and greater automation. The number of nonrequired filings is also expected to rise. The expanding number of operators and an active assignment market have resulted in an ever-increasing adjudicative workload in the Gulf of Mexico OCS Region. Management of the supplemental bonding program may become more complex with the growth in deepwater leasing and development.

Bid Evaluation

Detailed evaluation of individual tracts must be made to determine the potential fair market value of the tract for bid evaluation purposes. Prior to and immediately following a lease sale, the MMS identifies seismic data needed to evaluate bids on specific tracts. With industry's migration into the deeper water areas of the Gulf, bids are being received in areas where there is insufficient information for tract evaluation. Most of the deepwater areas where there is active industry interest are newly surveyed or are currently being surveyed. Regulations allow the MMS to acquire copies of this geophysical data for the cost of reproduction. A vast amount of data is expected to be needed to support of deepwater bid evaluation. A total 15,108 line-miles of 2D seismic data and 1,424 blocks of 3D seismic data was acquired to support the bid evaluation for Central Gulf Lease Sale 157 held in April 1996.

21

Previously, the high costs and risks associated with exploration and development of any single tract in water depths greater than 3,000 feet generally resulted in the determination that the tract had nominal fair market value. With deepwater royalty relief, the water depth range of economically viable tracts has shifted to deeper waters, adding many more tracts to the full bid evaluation workload. Many marginal prospects will become economically viable under royalty relief. To evaluate a tract that will obtain royalty relief on a unit or field basis, the evaluation must encompass the entire potential unit or field. These evaluations will usually encompass four to six tracts for every tract previously evaluated, greatly increasing the workload of the Region.

Reserves and Resource Evaluation

Reserves and resource estimates derived from geologic and engineering studies are used by many offices and sections within the Region. The type of evaluation for the vast majority of deepwater fields has been from the interpretation of conventional 2D seismic survey data and well data. The MMS will need to reevaluate these deepwater fields using state-of-the-art 3D seismic survey data to improve the interpretations and field analyses. The Gulf Region is in the initial stages of this evaluation. The advent of each new tool or method generates new ideas in the search for hydrocarbons. Computers can process raw geophysical and geological data at speeds that ten years ago would have been impossible to do in a lifetime. Computer evaluation of 3D seismic data has enabled the creation of three-dimensional subsurface interpretations. It is now possible to evaluate the configurations of subsurface horizons on a grid of a few feet instead of the conventional mile-by-mile grid of data. Analysis of actual seismic reflector characteristics can now be performed to estimate the thickness and geographic extent of reservoir rock and its fluid content. The increase in the detail of interpretations has led to the discovery of many hydrocarbon pools, discoveries that would not have been possible a few years ago. Armed with these new tools, explorationists can identify potential reservoirs in progressively deeper waters. Each advance in technology also requires continual training of MMS geologists, geophysicists, and engineers to keep abreast of the latest methods.

There are about 33,000 boreholes in the Gulf of Mexico. Some of the existing well data are unreliable and the process for correcting the well data is labor-intensive and difficult. Currently, MMS personnel make programmatic decisions based on well data that is a combination of hard copy records and historical data that resides in the TIMS database. Analyses made on the basis of questionable data can result in erroneous resource and reserve estimates, which can lead to later errors in decisions on fair market value and royalty relief. Over the next two years, the Gulf Region will systematically research and verify all historical well data and make the changes to the database.

The recent expansion in the size of the Gulf of Mexico lease sales has increased the regional mapping workload related to these sales. A comprehensive evaluation of the existing deepwater discoveries will need to be done on a field-wide basis, rather than on a single-block basis. Leases with new discoveries and the adjoining blocks need to be studied to determine both reserve and resource potential. These analyses will require a complete understanding and explanation of the field structure, stratigraphic setting, and boundaries. Evaluation of deepwater fields will require detailed geological, geophysical, and reservoir engineering analyses of about 800 additional blocks.

Deepwater field analyses provide analogs for fair market value determinations and will be used to evaluate whether leases meet the criteria for royalty relief established by the Deep Water Royalty Relief Act. Royalty relief evaluations will involve the modeling of digital geophysical data submitted with applications, conducting completeness reviews, running, verifying the acceptability of the engineering model inputs, and evaluating economic information submitted in connection with the Act.

Exploration, Development, and Production Activities

Exploration and Development Plans

Deepwater development is expected to increase the number of Exploration Plans (EP's), Supplemental EP's, and Development Operations Coordination Documents (DOCD's) submittals, and the workload involved in the review and analysis of these plans. Facilities proposed in these plans may be more complex and could incorporate new and unusual technologies. In addition, deepwater oil fields tend to have higher sulfur content. High-sulfur operations may require additional technical, safety, and environmental review. More than 400 deepwater leases will expire by the year 2000 unless they are drilled, unitized, or granted suspensions of operations. These pending expirations are anticipated to stimulate activity in the next four years.

The more complex and larger proposals for deepwater operations will require more extensive environmental reviews. By 1998, the number of environmental assessments and categorical exclusion reviews conducted by the Region could increase by as much as 50 percent and 30 percent, respectively. To a lesser extent, increases may also be anticipated in the numbers of oil spill response plan, archaeological, air quality, chemosynthetic community, and live bottom reviews conducted over the next several years. An Environmental Assessment (EA) must be prepared for any proposal involving the use of new and unusual technology. Environmental reviews must include multiple anchor sites as well as the structure's surface location, wider anchoring spreads, new and unusual technologies, and extensive oil-spill analyses. Chemosynthetic community surveys and reviews are required in water depths greater than 400 meters (1,312 feet). Impacts to endangered, threatened, and/or protected species may become an issue as development moves into deeper waters. Extended or large-volume flaring and oil or condensate burning associated with deepwater well testing will require full evaluation of impacts to air quality. Currently, environmental reviews are done for individual proposals, each of which may have little to no associated air emissions or water discharges. Projected centralized "host" production facilities will concentrate the air emissions and water discharges of several satellite completions at one location. Large production rates and volumes will also complicate environmental analyses.

Pipelines

Pipeline installation applications are anticipated to increase in numbers, as well as complexity. Additional production from more active leases and the fact that the pipeline infrastructure in many areas of the Gulf is at or near capacity will stimulate expansion of the pipeline system. Aging existing pipelines may require replacement pipelines to be installed to service both deepwater and shallow-water facilities. Many of the deepwater fields are located in areas where there is no existing pipeline infrastructure, so development will require new pipelines to shore. In addition, if the oil characteristics of new fields are incompatible with the oil in the existing pipeline systems or with separation/treatment facilities, new pipeline systems to shore will have to be installed. Deepwater pipelines will be longer and may require new technology for pipelaying and for transmission of the well production. In some cases, new technologies will require review for alternative compliance with OCS regulations. These longer pipelines have a greater potential of impacting environmental resources (e.g., prehistoric and historic archaeological resources, chemosynthetic communities, and topographic features). Longer pipelines may encounter more geologic hazards or ordnance disposal areas, which may require special safety systems or span analyses. The formation of hydrates and paraffins will be of concern because of the colder temperatures encountered at the seafloor in deepwater and may create the need for review and approval of additional injection systems or for insulated pipelines. Larger pipelines will require more complex oil-spill contingency plan reviews. New landfalls could add to impacts to coastal wetlands and habitats; each pipeline to shore will require a site-specific EA to address these issues. Any pipelines carrying oil or gas with high sulphur content may require additional technical, safety, and environmental review, and may require special mitigation. Many new pipelines servicing deepwater development have already been built and others are being proposed (see Figure 6).

Technical Review

Rapidly evolving and developing technical capabilities have enabled operations to move into deeper water. A number of technical considerations and concerns have been raised regarding deepwater development projects. For the MMS to be effective in its review and evaluation of deepwater operations, frequent meetings with operators, service vendors, and research entities are necessary to understand the technological developments.

Because operations and equipment used in deepwater are different from those used in shallower waters, the existing regulations, originally written for conventional, shallow-water operations, cannot be directly applied to proposed deepwater operations in many cases. For example, current regulations do not address the extended testing period that is often requested for deepwater wells. Safety device location, operation, and testing are fundamentally different for subsea completions that will be used in deepwater areas. Abandonment and site clearance procedures are expected to be significantly different for deepwater structures. Further, there is currently no review and approval process for transporting production by means other than by pipeline. As a result, the MMS has been granting variances from the regulations, as well as requiring adherence to new mitigation and safety measures unique to deepwater operations.

Requiring the submittal of a Deepwater Operations Plan (DWOP) (Notice to Lessees [NTL] 96-4N) was established to address the different functional requirements of equipment in deepwater, particularly the safety system requirements associated with subsea development systems, and the complexities and unique types of fixed and floating production facilities. The DWOP allows the MMS and industry to identify very early in the plan review process any potential issues specific to deepwater operations. The plans provide a mechanism for the coordination of permitting responsibilities within the MMS and also provide a mechanism for the consistent application of policies and regulations. Another reason for the DWOP is that deepwater technology is evolving faster than MMS's ability to revise OCS Operating Regulations. The NTL process is flexible enough to keep pace with the expanding activities and technology.

Currently, 27 existing regulations have been identified by the MMS and industry as requiring a departure or alternative compliance approval to permit development operations to proceed (see Table 7). For the MMS to grant alternative compliance approvals, the operator must demonstrate an equivalent or improved degree of safety. A departure can be granted when necessary if the operator can demonstrate that an acceptable level of safety exists. The MMS safety, technical, and engineering review of departure requests can be complex, involving risk assessment and a review of hazards analyses conducted by the operator. Requests for departure or alternative compliance are occurring more often as operations move into even deeper waters and the use of new technologies is proposed.

Figure 6. Major New Deepwater Oil and Gas Pipelines 1995-1996 (map)

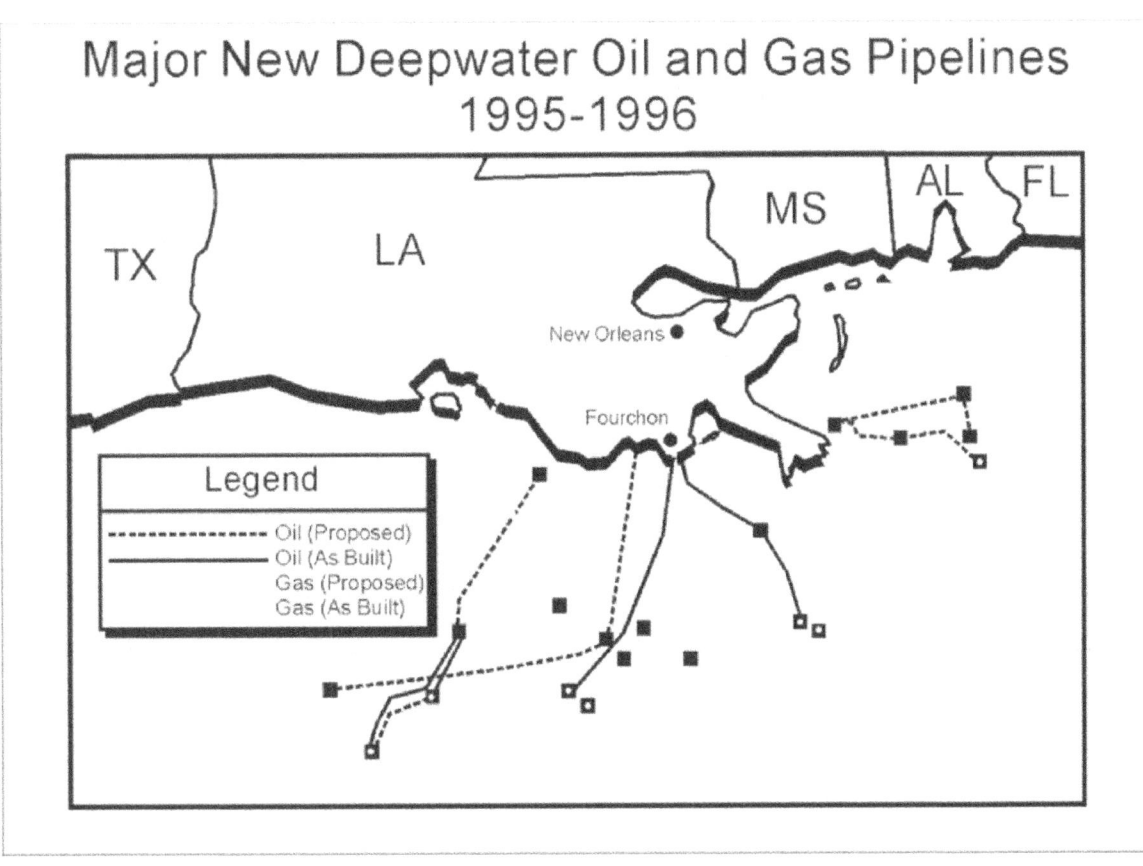

Table 7. Typical Departures/Alternative Compliance for Deepwater Projects

MMS Regulation	Departure/Alternative Compliance
250.51(h)	Emergency shut down station installed near the driller's console.
250.57(e)(3)	BOP equipment testing interval
250.87(c)	Casing annuli monitoring requirement
250.87(d)	Pressure rating of tree, wellhead, and related equipment (SITP vs. SCSSV operating pressure)
250.107(d)	Pressure rating of tree, wellhead, and related equipment
250.112(I)	Permanent abandonment of wells - clearance of location
250.113	- Temporary abandonment of wells
250.121(e)(4)	- SCSSV installation, maintenance, and testing requirements
250.121(I)	- Closure of SCSSV in response to ESD (and fire detection system activation requirements)
250.122(b)	Subsea flowline FSV requirements (ref: API RP 14C A1.2(b)(2) and Figure A.1.2)
250.122(d)	USV installation, maintenance, and test requirements
250.123(b)(2)(I)	PSHL set point requirements (for subsea pressure sensors)
250.123(b)(2)(ii)	Flowline and valve working pressure requirements
250.123(b)(4)(ii)	USV and SCSSV closure time requirements
250.123(b)(11)	Erosion control program requirements
250.124(a)(1)(I)	SCSSV function and leak test (interval and criteria)
250.124(a)(3)(I)	PSHL device test requirements (interval for subsea pressure sensors)
250.124(a)(3)(iii)	SDV operations test requirement (interval)
250.124(a)(4)	USV leak test requirements (interval and criteria)
250.124(a)(5)	Subsea FSV leak test requirements (interval and criteria)
250.124(a)(10)	ESD operation test requirements (interval and USV/SCSSV closure)
250.126	Safety and Pollution Prevention equipment quality assurance requirements
250.152(a)	DOI pipelines internal design pressure calculation (e.g., use external pressure)
250.152(b)	Pipeline valves, flanges and fitting requirements (e.g., cold temperature effects)
250.154(b)(6)	Subsea tie-in FSV requirements
250.156(a)(1)	Abandonment requirements for DOI pipelines
250.174	Bottomhole pressure survey requirements

The MMS's Technology Assessment and Research Program (TARP) promotes safety of operations and prevention of oil spills and air pollution through the use of Best Available and Safest Technologies (BAST). The Program's objectives are to provide a continuing and comprehensive technology base within the MMS to ensure that OCS operations are orderly, safe, and pollution-free; to ensure that MMS regulatory requirements facilitate the use of advanced technologies; to provide leadership to industry, through research participation and dialogue at the engineering level; and to assure compliance with the provisions of OCSLA Section 21(b) that requires the Best Available and Safest Technologies (BAST). To meet these objectives in relation to deepwater development, the TARP has funded projects (see Table 8) in the following areas: (1) fluid/structure interactions; (2) fatigue life and reliability of a wide variety of deepwater facilities; (3) operational developments relative to pipelines and (4) behavior of oil spilled in deepwater blowouts and assessment of possible countermeasures. The TARP has been a catalyst in forming joint industry projects to address critical and emerging problems.

It is anticipated that the workload and budgetary impact of the anticipated deepwater development in the Gulf of Mexico on the TARP will be relatively minor. If the research requirements expand significantly, however, there may be some additional budget resources required as well as increased TARP staff workload to design and manage needed research projects.

Unitization

The number of applications for exploratory/development units is expected to increase significantly as a result of deepwater leasing and activities. In 1992, 11 percent of the unitization applications received were for deepwater units; in 1996, 84 percent of the applications were for deepwater units. Proposed deepwater units will likely require lengthier and more involved evaluations because they are usually larger in size (include more blocks) than shallow-water units. Units in shallow water commonly range in size from 1 to 4 leases per unit (84% of new shallow-water units applied for during 1992-1996). More than 50 percent of the deepwater units applied for during the same period contained 5 or more leases. Two deepwater units are bigger than 15 leases (a 16-lease unit at 1,200 meters water depth and a 19-lease unit at 1,400 meters water depth).

Because of the lag time in the development of technologies to drill in deepwater and the shortage of rigs capable of drilling in these areas, many deepwater leases will reach the end of their initial lease term without having been drilled, and so the leases could expire. To extend the term of an undrilled lease, the lessee may apply for a suspension of operations (SOO), or the lease may be included within an approved unit where drilling will occur. As there are many restrictions on granting an SOO, some operators may apply for unitization of an unreasonably large unit. Drilling on one lease within a unit holds all leases contributing acreage to the unit. Operators may also propose larger units to justify the high cost of deepwater development. The MMS must evaluate these larger proposed units in detail to ensure that unitization will meet MMS's goal of expediting oil and gas exploration and development. It is common for the MMS to include project-specific restrictions in the unit agreement, such as clauses to drop leases from the unit if exploratory drilling does not occur in a timely manner.

Table 8. Technology Assessment and Research Program Contracts and Cooperative Agreements to Support Deepwater Development

Project	Contractor/Organization	Estimated Cost
Well Control Procedures - research needed to avoid blowouts in deepwater where drilling relief wells is extremely difficult	Louisiana State University	$280,000
Offshore Composites Engineering & Application Center - research on increasing strength and reducing weight in composite materials	Joint Industry Project (JIP) with University of Houston	$20,000
International Workshop on the Use of composites in Offshore Operations (see above)	JIP/ with University of Houston	$50,000
International Workshop on Advanced Materials	JIP/Colorado School of Mines	$80,000
Methods to Control Hydrates for Deepwater Operations - research related to lower temperatures and higher pressures found in deepwater operating environments, which causes more rapid development of these undesirable compounds	JIP/Westport Technology	$50,000
Control of Paraffins for Deepwater Operations (see above)	JIP/University of Texas	$100,000
Integrity of Deepwater Pipelines - research into welding and other improvements in laying deepwater pipelines	JIP/University of Texas	$75,000
Deepwater Offshore Technology Research Center - a test facility to model forces acting on deepwater structures and pipe lines, as well as a center to support offshore technology research	Texas A & M University	$50,000
Analysis of Oil Spill Behavior and Countermeasures for Subsea Oil Well Blowouts	S.L. Ross Environmental Research Ltd.	$15,000

Deepwater Royalty Relief

Deepwater royalty relief will create significant new workloads for most offices in the Gulf Region. There will be the additional workload of handling royalty relief applications and associated application fees. Each royalty relief request will require review and analysis of block-specific and/or field-specific bathymetric, geological, and geophysical data and information. Block-specific bathymetric data will need to be incorporated into the TIMS/GIS database. The workload associated with MMS field determinations will expand in response to the requirements of the Deep Water Royalty Relief Act--e.g., earlier delineation of the entire potential field (undrilled leases and unleased acreage, as well as the leases included in the field or unit); greater utilization of 3D seismic data; and appeals of initial determinations by lessees. Because deepwater royalty relief has just been implemented, unanticipated problems and issues will probably occur.

Deepwater royalty relief affects the data management and audit functions within the Royalty Management Program (RMP). Royalty suspension volumes are a new approach to royalty relief and minor changes will be required to RMP's automated systems. These changes can be accommodated within the existing operation and maintenance activities. The Gulf Region and RMP are working jointly to develop an efficient procedure to monitor production from leases subject to suspension volumes to ensure that royalty payments commence at the proper time. Finally, RMP will audit some of the royalty relief applications prior to granting relief. A complete application currently requires certification by a Certified Public Accountant regarding the accuracy of historic costs included as a basis for royalty relief. RMP will use these certifications to evaluate whether an audit is necessary. It's too soon to accurately estimate the workload associated with these audits.

Conservation

Conservation, which is ensuring that economic reserves are fully developed and produced, is an increasingly important part of the Region's workload. Industry requests related to conservation issues include both routine and nonroutine requests (see Table 9). Routine requests require a minimum amount of effort beyond entry of the data into the Regional database for tracking and monitoring purposes. Nonroutine requests include those that involve a departure from normal operating parameters or requests when there is a suspected violation of the regulations. Nonroutine requests generally require more intensive review. Deepwater conservation reviews are a new element of MMS regulatory responsibilities that will require extensive studies; they therefore are treated as nonroutine requests. Greater numbers of both routine and nonroutine requests are expected from the incremental increase of producing leases and wells in the deepwater Gulf of Mexico.

The MMS has developed a new conservation initiative for conventional projects in water depths greater than or equal to 1,000 feet, and for all subsea completion projects regardless of water depth. The Gulf Region established requirements for the submission of Conservation Information through the issuance of NTL 96-6N, effective October 1, 1996. Conservation reviews will be more complex and economically sensitive in deepwater areas. Because of higher operating costs in deepwater, operators may be more reluctant to produce smaller oil-bearing strata prior to production of associated gas caps. In addition, in an attempt to improve cash flow, more operators are requesting to produce oil-bearing strata and gas caps simultaneously. Downhole commingling (producing from more than one reservoir in the same completion) may be crucial to the development of deepwater projects because deepwater fields may be economically producible only if production from several reservoirs occurs simultaneously. There is a need for approval of longer well testing durations in deepwater, sometimes 1-2 weeks or even longer, in order to justify the huge costs of deepwater development. These extended tests result in requests for larger volumes of gas flaring and burning of liquid hydrocarbons. At the same time, barging of test liquids becomes problematic in the rough, deepwater seas. The number of bottomhole pressure survey waiver requests rose dramatically in deeper water, largely due to the frequency of subsea completions. As the number of such requests increases with deepwater development and the extent of these requests pushes the existing regulations to their limits, there will be need for greater scrutiny and more detailed analyses when these requests are reviewed.

Table 9. Routine and Nonroutine Conservation Requests

	FY 1992	FY 1993	FY 1994	FY 1995	FY 1996
Routine					
Bottomhole Pressure Tests	2,111	1,829	1,435	1,192	1,521
MER Data Entry	1,045	831	777	873	824
Well Potential and Semiannual Tests	23,123	22,660	19,820	14,920	15,140
Total Routine	26,279	25,320	22,032	16,985	17,485
Nonroutine					
Bottomhole Pressure Test Waivers	35	31	39	6	32
Gas Cap Production Requests	13	14	21	32	48
Reservoir Reclassification	10	8	2	5	4
Lease Assignment for Supplemental Bonding Requests	14	45	55	42	34
Deepwater Conservation Reviews	0	0	0	0	9
Sensitive/Downhole Commingling Requests	9	6	8	10	12
Gas Flaring Requests	215	320	349	344	377
Downhole Commingling Requests	60	107	103	121	123
500 Feet From Lease Line Requests	16	13	15	21	24
Total Nonroutine	372	544	592	581	663

The MMS Gulf Region is establishing two new work activities for deepwater development. First, all relevant, available data, such as well logs, seismic data, isopach maps, cross sections, etc., will be reviewed in order to evaluate whether all economically producible reservoirs penetrated are to be developed and produced. If the MMS identifies producible zones that were not included in the operator's development plan, the MMS will require the operator to provide justification as to why these reservoirs are not to be produced. Second, all requests to abandon completions will also be reviewed to ensure that completions are not prematurely abandoned before all economically producible reserves are recovered. These reviews were established in response to the extremely high costs associated with deepwater operations. High operating costs may create some pressure or incentive for operators to bypass or to abandon smaller, economically producible reserves in order to move to larger, more profitable reservoirs.

Inspection and Enforcement

The recent deepwater discoveries are 100-200 miles from shore base, and flight times may be as much as 3-4 hours round trip. (The average distance and flight time to the more than 3,800 platforms operating in the Gulf are approximately 80 miles from shore base and 45-50 minutes of flight time.) Deepwater facilities will be larger and more complex, taking longer to inspect than the average shallower water structures. Inspections of deepwater facilities will require more trips, or overnight stays, to complete. This situation creates a need to bolster the Regional inspection force and helicopter fleet. Additional training will be required for both inspectors and engineers on new production systems, new technologies for deepwater drilling and production, and new procedures for inspections and accident investigations. The number of inspections conducted by the Region is expected to increase by 20 percent by FY98.

As more rigs become available for deepwater drilling operations, more of the MMS Districts' time will be spent reviewing and approving Applications for Permit to Drill and Sundry Notices. More inspection time will be devoted to inspecting these deepwater drilling and production operations.

Structure Removal and Site Clearance

Structure removal and site clearance for deepwater structures may present additional environmental concerns and new technological and regulatory challenges. Because of higher structure removal costs, industry is expected to request approvals for mid-water abandonments, leaving lower sections of decommissioned structures that have little or no environmental benefits as artificial reefs. Department of Defense issues, disposal at sea, and liability issues will need to be addressed.

Other Workload Factors

The OCS Program in the Gulf of Mexico is thriving--presenting challenges and expanding workload in all aspects of the activities. During FY95, there were approximately 5,000 active leases in the Gulf of Mexico Region; in January 1997 this had reached 6,177 active leases; and by FY98 this number is expected to exceed 8,300 active leases, a 40 percent increase. More independent companies are becoming active in the offshore Gulf of Mexico; some have little or no experience with MMS rules and policies.

The increase in deepwater development and associated complexities in the technical, safety, and environmental reviews of deepwater exploration and development projects is occurring at a time when the shelf infrastructure is also undergoing a transition. Existing offshore infrastructure is also approaching (and in some instances surpassing) its design life, necessitating additional attention to ensure that operations can be conducted in a safe manner.

Monitoring environmental mitigation, both for operator compliance and for the effectiveness of the mitigating measures, is an increasingly important part of the MMS mission. Baseline studies and assessment of environmental impacts are necessary for the MMS to develop effective mitigation measures. The Oil Pollution Act of 1990 gave the MMS new responsibilities in overseeing oil-spill prevention and contingency planning. Bonding requirements for offshore operators were revised, and the MMS is responsible for ensuring legal compliance with the new requirements.

Increasing OCS activities require increasing coordination with Federal, State, and local agencies. The MMS Gulf Region is actively involved in several cooperative efforts with other Federal agencies. The MMS is cooperating with the Environmental Protection Agency in monitoring compliance with more restrictive water pollution controls, and MMS inspectors have assumed new duties in collecting water samples from offshore platforms and performing more visual inspections for discharged effluents. The Federal Energy Regulatory Commission (FERC) will use MMS's EA for a pipeline east of the Mississippi delta as the base document for the preparation of the FERC EIS on the project. The MMS and the Department of Transportation (DOT) have entered into a Memorandum of Understanding (MOU) ensuring that all producer's pipelines are under MMS regulatory jurisdiction and transportation pipelines remain under DOT's jurisdiction. This MOU significantly increases the miles of pipelines under MMS's jursidiction.

Operations in the Gulf are expanding in directions other than just into deeper waters. There are a tremendous number of supplemental plans being submitted to drill additional wells from existing facilities. Many of these supplemental plans are for wells to develop production from subsalt plays or previously undeveloped shallow reservoirs, horizontal wells, and multi-lateral wells. Exploration activities and possible development operations in the Eastern Gulf of Mexico Planning Area will require a comprehensive Environmental Impact Statement to evaluate the potential impact of OCS operations in this frontier area. Potential sand mining in the Central Gulf of Mexico is looming on the horizon and will require detailed environmental assessment and new expertise. Similar activities may occur in the Atlantic Region, which is now under the jurisdiction of the Gulf of Mexico Regional Office. Alternative transportation of OCS production, such as tankering, is being considered for operations both in shallow and deepwater areas. These operations will also require extensive environmental, safety and technical review. To facilitate oil spill analyses, the Gulf Region is formulating requirements for submitting information about storage tanks on offshore facilities. Legal challenges and coastal zone consistency determinations, as well as public education and outreach, will also consume increasing amounts of staff time.

Summary

As a result of technological advances that have proven successful in field application, new discoveries, and the recent passage of the Deep Water Royalty Relief Act, there is renewed industry interest in Gulf of Mexico deepwater leasing. The challenges of effectively managing and regulating exploration and development activities in the frontier deepwater areas are in addition to ever-increasing demands of the OCS Program in the shallower water areas of the Gulf. The impacts on the workload and demands on the Minerals Management Service, particularly the Gulf of Mexico OCS Regional Office, as a result of deepwater activities are just beginning. Although some specific impacts are emerging and others can be anticipated, the full magnitude of the impacts is not yet known. Deepwater development will impact all aspects of the MMS Gulf Region's Program--from geological and geophysical permitting and prelease environmental analysis, through conducting lease sales, evaluating exploration and development plans, and conducting inspections, to decommissioning structures and site clearance.

Appendix 1. Deepwater Activity Indicators

Indicator	1992	1993	1994	1995	1996
Prelease Stage					
Geological & Geophysical Permits Issued	11	14	11	12	38
Leasing Stage					
Lease Sales (Central Planning Area/Western Planning Area)	139/141	142/143	147/150	152/155	157/161
Blocks Offered (total blocks/ deepwater blocks)	9,618/ 7,019	10,125/ 7,188	10,861/ 7,507	10,991/ 7,609	5,649/ 5,168
Blocks Bid On (total blocks/ deepwater blocks)	212/ 24	358/ 62	585/ 69	863/ 278	1,541/ 835
% Deepwater Tracts of Tracts Receiving Bids	11%	17%	12%	32%	54%
Leases Awarded (total leases/ deepwater leases)	204/ 24	336/ 60	560/ 69	835/ 274	1,508/ 822
% Deepwater Tracts of Tracts Leased	12%	18%	12%	33%	55%
Water Depth of Deepest Existing Lease (Year End)	2,850 m	2,740 m	2,740 m	2,740 m	2,850 m
Plans and Permit Stage					
Exploration Plans (New) Submitted to MMS	13	13	21	20	23
Exploration Plans Approved by MMS	14	12	16	14	22
Development Plans (New) Submitted to MMS	2	3	2	5	4
Development Plans Approved by MMS	2	2	2	5	4

Appendix 1. Deepwater Activity Indicators *(continued)*

Indicator	1992	1993	1994	1995	1996
Applications for Permit to Drill Approved by MMS	39	41	66	85	126
Drilling Stage					
Rigs Drilling - Monthly Average	3	6	11	14	19
Rigs Drilling - Peak Number Drilling Simultaneously/Month	6	9	15	20	26
Production Stage					
Water Depth of Deepest Structure[1] (feet)	1,720	1,720	2,860	2,860	2,940
Number of Fields in Production	6	8	12	14	16[2]
Total Production from Deepwater Fields/Year (MMBO/Bcf)	37.4/ 94.0	37.4/ 133.8	42.7/ 177.8	57.4/ 212.4	n/a
Total Number of Designated Fields (Active and Expired)	61	65	70	76	85[2]
Reserves Stage					
Total Number of Deepwater Fields with Proven Reserves	15	15	18	20	25[2]
Total Proved Reserves in Deepwater Fields (MMBLS/Tcf)	844/ 2.6	813/ 2.9	1,132/ 4.1	1,132/ 4.6	1,370[2]/ 4.92[2]

[1] 1992-93 Conoco's Jolliet TLP in GC 184
1994-95 Shell's Auger TLP in GB 426
1996 Shell's Mars TLP in MC 807
[2] As of June 1996

Appendix 2. Deepwater Production and Discoveries

Prospect Name	Operator (Partners)	Area/ Block	Water Depth (feet)	Discovery Announced	Estimated Production Start-up	Platform/ System Type	Distance from New Orleans (miles)
Allegheny	Enserch (Mobil, Reading & Bates)	GC254	3,186			FPS	155
Amberjack*	BP (Shell, Conoco)	MC109	1,029	1989	1991	fixed	102
Auger*	Shell (BP)	GB426	2,860	1987	1994	TLP	219
Baldpate	Amerada Hess	GB260	1,641	1995	1998	compliant tower	191
Bison	Exxon	GC166	2,518				149
Boomvang	Reading & Bates	EB688	3,737			subsea	328
Brutus	Shell (Exxon)	GC158	2,877	1995			152
Bullwinkle*	Shell	GC62	1,353	1985	1989	fixed	153
Cognac*	Shell	MC194	1,025	1976	1979	fixed	101
Cooper*	Enserch (EP Operating)	GB388	2,190		1995	FPS	206
Coulomb	Shell	MC657	7,500				170
Diamond	Oryx	MC445	2,095			subsea	103
Diana	Exxon (BP)	EB945	4,400	1991	unknown	unknown	356

Appendix 2. Deepwater Production and Discoveries (continued)

Prospect Name	Operator (Partners)	Area/ Block	Water Depth (feet)	Discovery Announced	Estimated Production Start-up	Platform/ System Type	Distance from New Orleans (miles)
Europa	BP	MC935	3,889				139
Fuji	Texaco (Shell)	GC506	4,243	1995	2000	known	178
Gemini	Texaco (Chevron)	MC292	3,393	1995	2000	unknown	125
Genesis	Chevron (Exxon, Fina)	GC205	2,597	1996	1998	spar	153
Jolliet*	Conoco	GC184	1,720		1989	TLP	174
King	Amoco	MC84	5,500				145
Kings Peak	Amoco	DC133	6,530		2000		153
Lena*	Exxon	MC281	1,018		1983	guyed tower	105
Macaroni	Shell	GB602	3,600				228
Marlin	Amoco	VK915	3,236		2000		141
Mars*	Shell (BP)	MC807	2,940	1989	1996	TLP/ subsea	134
Mensa	Shell	MC687	5,376	1995	1997	subsea	144
Mickey	Exxon (BP)	MC211	4,356	1991	unknown	unknown	137

Appendix 2. Deepwater Production and Discoveries (continued)

Prospect Name	Operator (Partners)	Area/ Block	Water Depth (feet)	Discovery Announced	Estimated Production Start-up	Platform/ System Type	Distance from New Orleans (miles)
Morpeth	British-Borneo	EW965	1,630			Seastar TLP / subsea	134
Neptune	Oryx	VK826	1,930		1997	spar	136
No name	Shell	MC522	6,950				157
No name	Shell	MC429	6,274				142
No name	BP	MC718	2,828				127
No name	Chevron	GB254	1,920				202
No name	Texaco	GB269	1,102				268
No name	Shell	GC69	1,465				147
No name	Mobil	GC 72	1,655			subsea	147
No name	Texaco	GC228	1,638				177
No name	Shell	MC383	5,759				136
No name	Conoco	GC472	3,817				170
No name	BP	MC26	1,272				109
No name	BP	AV575	6,220				179
No name	Conoco (Oryx)	MC 243	3,100		2000		113

41

Appendix 2. Deepwater Production and Discoveries (*continued*)

Prospect Name	Operator (Partners)	Area/ Block	Water Depth (feet)	Discovery Announced	Estimated Production Start-up	Platform/ System Type	Distance from New Orleans (miles)
No name	BP	MC162	3,414				124
No name	Enserch (Agip, Fina)	MC441	1,520			subsea	101
Oyster	Marathon (Texaco)	EW917	1,200	1996	1997	subsea	131
Petronius	Texaco (Marathon)	VK786	1,754	1995	1999	compliant tower	146
Pompano II*	BP (Kerr-McGee)	MC28	1,865		1995	subsea	113
Pompano I*	BP (Kerr-McGee)	VK989	1,290	1991	1994	fixed	109
Popeye*	Shell (CNG, Mobil, BP)	GC116	2,000	1985	1996	subsea	148
Ram-Powell	Shell (Exxon, Amoco)	VK956	3,255	1995	1997	TLP	135
Rocky*	Shell	GC110	1,785	1996	1996	subsea	152
Seattle Slew*	Tatham	EW914	920	1991	1993	subsea	131
Shasta*	Texaco (Hardy & Samedan)	GC136	1,040	1994	1995	subsea	178

Appendix 2. Deepwater Production and Discoveries (continued)

Prospect Name	Operator (Partners)	Area/ Block	Water Depth (feet)	Discovery Announced	Estimated Production Start-up	Platform/ System Type	Distance from New Orleans (miles)
Spend-A-Buck*	Flextrend (Mid-Con)	GB117	940	1994	1996	subsea	206
Sunday Silence	Tatham	EW958	1,450	1994	1998	Truss spar	134
Tahoe II*	Shell (Murphy)	VK 783	1,500	1984	1996	subsea	138
Tahoe*	Shell (Murphy)	VK783	1,500	1984	1994	subsea	138
Troika	BP (Shell, Marathon)	GC244	2,721	1994	1998	subsea	159
Ursa	Shell (Exxon, BP, Conoco)	MC809	4,021	1996	1999	TLP	136
VK 862*	Walter	VK862	1,043		1995	subsea	116
Zinc*	Exxon	MC354	1,478		1993	subsea	95

* Indicates prospect currently on production.

43